FISH

goldfish

NATIONAL GEOGRAPHIC NATURE LIBRARY

FISH

NATIONAL GEOGRAPHIC NATURE LIBRARY

by Elizabeth Schleichert

NATIONAL GEOGRAPHIC SOCIETY

Washington, D.C.

All photographs supplied by
Animals Animals/Earth Scenes

longnose hawkfish

Table of Contents

clown triggerfish

Atlantic salmon

spotted eagle ray

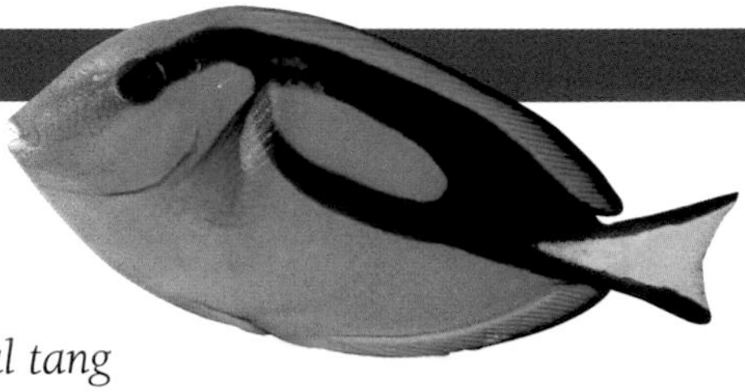

regal tang

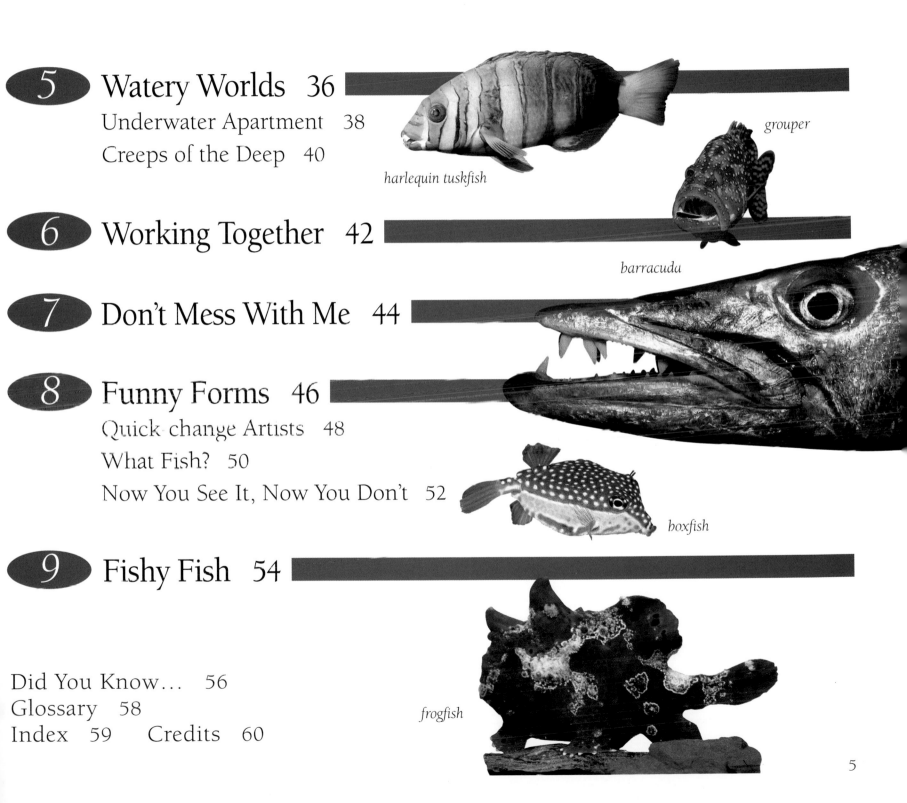

grouper

harlequin tuskfish

barracudu

boxfish

frogfish

WHAT IS A FISH?

Nearly every body of water supports fish. They vary more in size and shape than any other type of animal in the world. There are more than 20,000 kinds of fish. They are divided into three main groups: jawless fish; sharks and their relatives; and bony fish.

Fish have certain things in common:

- They are AQUATIC (ah-KWAT-ik), which means they live in the water.
- They are VERTEBRATES (VURT-uh-bruts).
- They take in oxygen through GILLS.
- Most fish are COLD-BLOODED.
- Most have FINS.
- Most have SCALES.

leopard shark

silver hatchetfish

flame angelfish

yellowtail snapper

golden trout

golden butterfly fish

juvenile ribbon eel

fairy basslets

clearnose skate

panther grouper

7

Fins Are Fine

There are so many different kinds of fish that it is hard to describe a typical one. Like this largemouth bass, most fish—but not all of them—have scales. These are hard, thin plates that form a fish's outer layer. Every fish has a head, a body, and a tail. Most have fins for swimming and gills for taking in oxygen from the water.

dorsal fin

A fish takes in water through its mouth.

Beneath the gill cover, or operculum (oh-PER-kyu-lum), lie the gills and gill openings. Water passes over the gills and out the gill openings. Blood vessels in the gills absorb oxygen from the water, and blood carries the oxygen to the rest of the fish's body.

pectoral fin

Most fish have two sets of paired fins, the pectoral and pelvic. They usually use these fins for maneuvering or steering.

pelvic fin

dorsal fin

In most fish the tail fin provides power. Most fish swish their tails back and forth to swim.

The dorsal fins and the anal fin of a fish help keep it from tipping over.

Beneath its skin, a fish has a fluid-filled tube, or canal, along each side of its body. This is called the lateral line. The lateral line helps a fish sense movements in the water, alerting it to nearby danger or prey.

tail fin

anal fin

9

Vertebrate Kin

You have more in common with fish than you would guess. Like you, fish are vertebrates—animals with backbones. Fish were the very first vertebrates on earth. They were here for more than 400 million years before the first humans arrived. All vertebrates, including mammals like you, trace their ancestry back to fish. Most fish need to live in the water and have streamlined bodies that help them move through the water.

WHALE OF A FISH
The world's largest fish, the whale shark swims lazily through the world's warm waters. Despite its size—nearly half the length of a basketball court—the whale shark is a gentle giant, harmless to people.

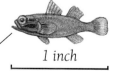

1 inch

The world's smallest fish, a tiny goby looks like a flea compared to a 40-foot-long whale shark.

RED FISH, BLUE FISH

To make these transparent glassfish more colorful, people have treated them with harmless liquids that highlight their backbones.

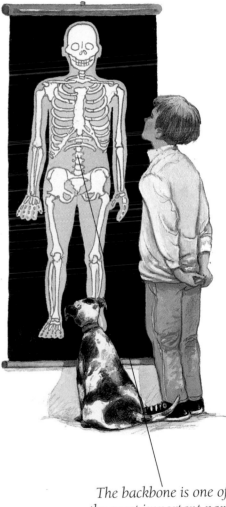

The backbone is one of the most important parts of a skeleton that supports the bodies of vertebrates.

11

Fresh Fish

About 8,000 kinds of fish live in the world's fresh waters—such as lakes, rivers, and ponds. Fish dwell in one mountain lake more than 12,000 feet above sea level. Others swim in the underground waters of caves. More kinds of freshwater fish live in the tropics than elsewhere in the world. The Amazon River in South America has 1,500 different varieties.

OLD FAVORITE
The world's most popular pet fish, goldfish come in various shades of red and white. Most are reddish orange, and some are speckled.

Bred by people for more than 1,000 years, goldfish are descended from giant carp-like fish that live in Asia.

MINISCULE MINNOW
The white-cloud mountain minnow of China measures only an inch and a half long. Minnows live in fresh waters worldwide.

Its greenish hue helps the mountain minnow blend into a streambed.

Long, cat-like "whiskers," called barbels (BAR-buls), gave the catfish its name. Catfish live in fresh waters of every continent except Antarctica.

ONE IN A MILLION ▶
Native to the West Indies and South America, the dazzling guppy thrives in aquariums. It was once called the "millions fish" because it produces so many offspring.

Some Like It Salty

More than 12,000 kinds of fish swim in the earth's saltwater oceans and seas. Most live along coasts, where food is plentiful, but some dwell in total darkness on the ocean floor. Others swim in the frigid Antarctic seas. Cold-water fish have a protein antifreeze in their blood—a fishy version of the fluid we put in our car radiators in winter.

STAY TUNA-ED
The bluefin tuna courses quickly through the open seas. Its top speed is 50 mph. Long-distance travelers, tuna often swim all the way across the Atlantic or Pacific Oceans.

A remora's sucker disk is actually a specialized dorsal fin.

GOIN' MY WAY?
The remora often hitches a ride on larger fish, clinging to its host with a special sucker disk on its head.

A sleek swimming machine, the bluefin tuna has a torpedo shape that makes for speed.

CORAL CLOWN

Flashy coral reef dweller, the clown triggerfish has a spine hidden in a dorsal fin on its back. When danger threatens, the triggerfish pops up the spine and wedges itself into a crevice.

The clown triggerfish has powerful teeth and jaws. These help the fish nibble hard-shelled snacks, such as sea urchins.

MOONLIGHT MADNESS

On high-tide nights in spring and summer, California grunions come ashore. The female wriggles into the sand and deposits her eggs. The male fertilizes them. When the next high tide swooshes in about two weeks later, out pop the young grunions.

What is Not a Fish

The waters of the world are teeming with creatures of all sorts. You might mistake some of them for fish, but don't be fooled. Even a creature with the word "fish" in its name may prove to be a pretender, not a true fish.

The sea star can perform a neat trick. If it loses an arm, it simply grows a new one.

STAR BRIGHT

Scientists now prefer the name "sea star" for the five-armed ocean dwellers once called starfish. Sea stars aren't fish at all. They have no backbones.

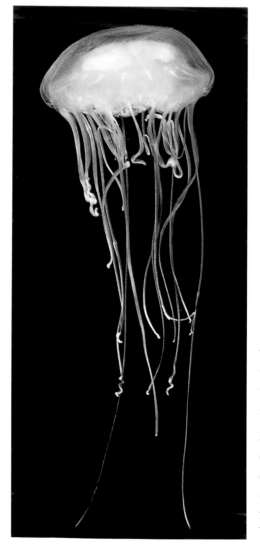

DON'T MEDDLE WITH THE NETTLE

The sea nettle may look harmless, but its long tentacles are armed with stinging cells that help it capture prey. A kind of jellyfish, the sea nettle lacks a backbone.

When an octopus finds a tasty morsel such as a clam, it uses suckers on its tentacles to pull the shellfish apart. Like a jellyfish, an octopus has no backbone.

The European crayfish is shy. It hides under stones in streams or ponds. A crayfish has a hard shell instead of scales and a backbone.

AIR BREATHER

Bottlenose dolphins are sea mammals, kin to whales. Like all mammals, dolphins breathe air. They surface every few minutes and draw air in through a blowhole on the top of their heads.

COLORFUL CRAWDADDY

Found the world over in fresh waters, crawdads or crayfish look like small lobsters. Most are brownish green, but some are red, white, pink, and even blue.

The Cycle of Life

Like all animals, fish reproduce regularly. Most reproduce, or spawn, once or twice a year, but some tropical fish reproduce all year-round. Spawning usually involves a male releasing his milt, or sperm, over a female's newly laid eggs. Some fish spawn in open waters. Cod may deposit three million eggs in the open sea. Many freshwater fish spawn in nests scooped from the bottom of lakes or streams. Eventually, the young hatch from the eggs. Some kinds of fish, such as certain sharks, give birth to live young.

TROUT JAMBOREE
Male and female brook trout come together before spawning. They swim to a protected spot and split up into mating pairs.

female trout lays as many as a thousand ggs in her redd.

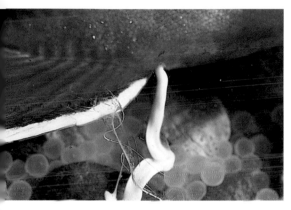

he male trout releases milt that covers e eggs and fertilizes them so that they an develop.

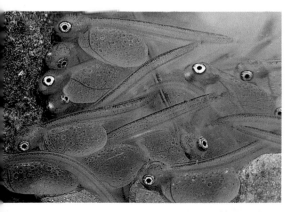

ach brook trout hatchling is born with a ulging yolk sac attached to its underside. he sac is like a take-along snack pack lled with food.

NEAT NESTERS

Brook trout, found in cool streams and lakes, breed by laying eggs in a nest, called a redd. At the spawning site, the female brook trout digs a nest. The male stands guard nearby, on the lookout for predators or rival fish.

BROOK TROUT BABIES

Brook trout hatchlings are called alevins (AL-eh-vins). Within 2 to 16 weeks, an alevin uses all the food in its yolk sac. Then it has to find its own food. Each alevin swims around searching for its favorite meal—a mouthful of tasty insects.

Have Fins, Will Travel

Fish are on the move a lot, swimming in search of food or to escape enemies. But some kinds *really* travel, migrating thousands of miles to mate or breed. On travels long and short, certain kinds of fish always move in a group, called a school. Traveling in numbers helps protect them from enemies. Other fish come together only to breed.

LONG-DISTANCE MOVE
The Atlantic salmon spends most of its adult life at sea. At spawning time, when it is three to nine years old, the salmon heads inland. Navigating by memory and smell, it makes its way up the stream where it was born, often leaping over waterfalls and other obstacles. Some salmon return to the sea, but many are so weak that they die on that return journey.

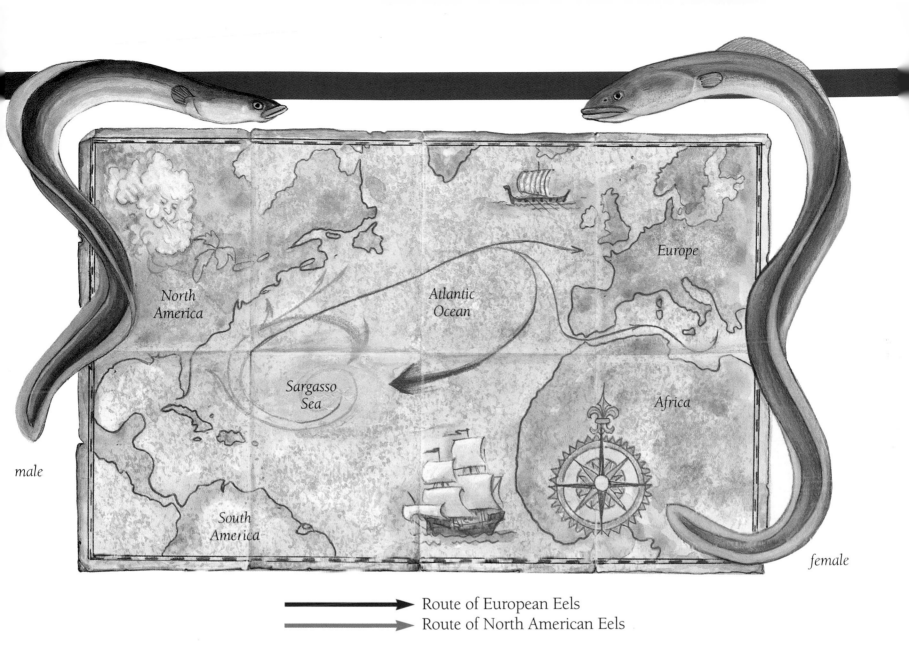

male

female

Route of European Eels
Route of North American Eels

TIRELESS TRAVELERS

The freshwater eel is an awesome traveler. Adults live in freshwater streams in both Europe and North America. At breeding time they head downstream and out to the Atlantic Ocean. They travel for a thousand or more miles to their birthplace in the Sargasso (sar-GAS-oh) Sea, an area of floating seaweed in the western Atlantic. During the journey, the eels don't eat. They face numerous challenges—hungry predators, violent storms, and fierce currents. Once in the Sargasso Sea, they breed and then die. Here, their tiny young are born. They measure only two or three inches long when they begin the incredible trip back to the freshwater streams of their parents. Once back in these streams, they develop into the eel equivalent of teenagers, called glass eels or elvers. Soon after they've arrived upstream, elvers become adults.

21

2 Jawless Wonders

Jawless fish have round mouths equipped with suckers instead of the jaws most fish have. Just two types of fish are jawless—lampreys and hagfish. They are the only surviving relatives of ancient jawless fish that swam in earth's oceans nearly 500 million years ago. The skeleton of a jawless fish is made of a flexible material called cartilage (KAR-tul-ij).

When a predator attacks, the hagfish ties a knot in its tail, works the knot up its body, then slips the knot over its head to escape the enemy's grasp.

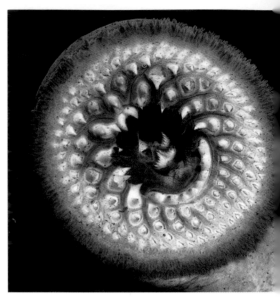

WHAT A SUCKER!
Up to 125 teeth line the sucker-like dis and mouth of a river lamprey. Its teeth help the lamprey clamp onto larger fish

WATER VAMPIRE ▶
A lamprey hitches itself to a brown trout, uses its teeth to dri a hole through the trout's scales, and dines on its victim's blood.

SLIME CENTRAL
Its body is so flexible that a hagfish can tie itself in knots. To keep enemies from stealing its food while it is dining, the hagfish oozes oodles of slippery slime that make it hard to grab. Its favorite food is dead fish.

Fossils show that the ostracoderm, ancestor of today's jawless fish, lived millions of years ago.

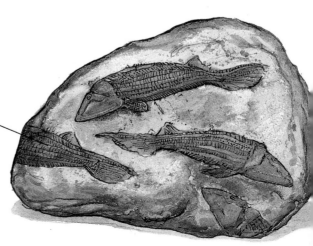

3 They've Got Jaws

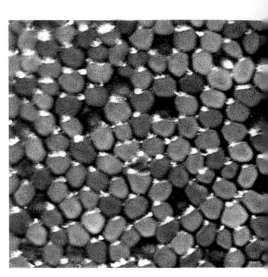

Sharks have been masters of the seas for millions of years, even before the time of dinosaurs. Their beady eyes give sharks a mean look, yet most of them are shy. Of the 375 kinds of sharks, only 30 are dangerous. Some sharks are as small as a person's hand; others are as big as a moving van. All sharks have jaws, and their skeletons are made of rubbery cartilage, not rigid bone. Like most fish, sharks swish their tails and bodies back and forth to glide through the water, but sharks can't back up, and they can't stop suddenly. Instead, they circle to change course.

SHARP SKIN
Small, pointed scales called denticles (DENT-ih-kuls) cover the skin of a shark. The denticles are rough and sharp.

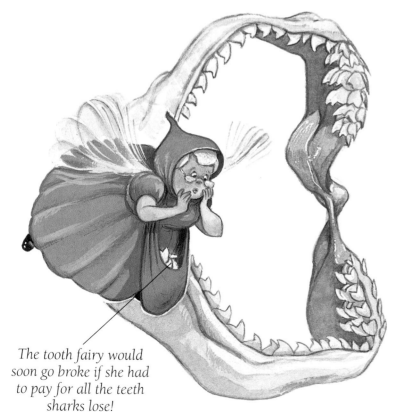

The tooth fairy would soon go broke if she had to pay for all the teeth sharks lose!

TOOTH FAIRY'S NIGHTMARE
A shark's jaws are lined with five or more rows of teeth, one behind the other. Those teeth are not set into its jaw, like yours, or like the teeth of bony fish. A shark's teeth are loosely attached to—even part of—the skin of the jaws. A shark's teeth fall out regularly when worn, but a new tooth moves forward to replace the lost one.

AMAZING EYES
A layer of reflecting cells in the back of a shark's eyes give it good vision in dim light.

Its snout, like the rest of a white shark's body, is streamlined for speed.

FIERCE HUNTER
Giving all sharks a bad rep, the white shark has attacked more people than any other kind of shark. Perhaps the white mistakes people for its usual prey—seals and sea lions.

The jaws of a white shark are powerful enough to bend a large boat propeller. The white snatches prey, then saws out a chunk of flesh with its razor-sharp teeth. More teeth, not visible in the photograph, line the shark's jaws.

25

Shark Portraits

Sharks come in many shapes and sizes and can be found in all the world's oceans, except those around Antarctica. Sharks are most common in tropical and subtropical seas. Sharks are survivors. They don't get many diseases, and they have few enemies.

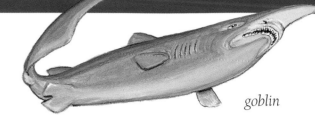

goblin

The hammerhead shark cruises the world's warm oceans in large schools.

HEADS UP!
Well named, the hammerhead is one of the strangest looking of all sharks. It has an eye on each end of its mallet-shaped head. As it swims, a hammerhead swings its head back and forth so that it can s a wide sweep of ocean. Buried within every shark's head are sense organs that pick up electrical signals given off by the shark's prey.

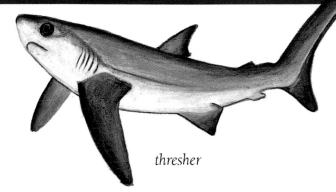

cookie cutter

thresher

SHAPES OF SHARKS

The goblin shark is like a ghost of the deep, seldom seen and rarely caught. A bite from a cookie-cutter shark leaves its mouth shape behind on its victim—usually a whale, seal, or dolphin. The thresher shark uses its tail, longest of any shark, as a whip to stun smaller fish.

FLOATING TRASHMAN

Not exactly a picky eater, the tiger shark is called the "garbage can of the sea." Stomachs of tiger sharks have held the remains of porpoises, fish, turtles, beef bones, tin cans, and fishnet floats. Tiger sharks are found worldwide in warm seas and are especially common in the waters off Australia and in the Caribbean. They are considered one of the most dangerous of all sharks.

Its spotted coloring helps conceal the carpet shark while it lies in wait for passing fish, crabs, and octopuses.

CARPET CRITTER

The wobbegong, or carpet shark, lies like a rug on the seafloor around coral reefs of Australia. When the carpet shark spots prey, it latches on with sharp, dagger-like teeth.

27

Cartilage Cousins

Sharks have more than 300 relatives. Among them are fish called rays and skates. Most rays and skates are diamond shaped and have skinny tails. They spend their time on the ocean floor. Half-buried in mud or sand, they hide from enemies or dig for crabs or worms. Like the skeletons of jawless fish and sharks, the skeletons of skates and rays are made of cartilage. These fish have especially large side, or pectoral, fins that are attached to their heads, making them look like underwater bats!

The sawfish, a cousin of ray uses its long snout to slash and stun fish. Lined with razor-like teeth, the "saw" co also wound an attacker.

What look like a skate's eyes are really its nostrils. The eyes of a skate are on the top of its head.

OUTER SPACE CRITTER
A friendly alien? Guess again. It's the bottom of a clearnose skate. The skate's mouth juts out from its body and helps it grab shellfish and other delicacies.

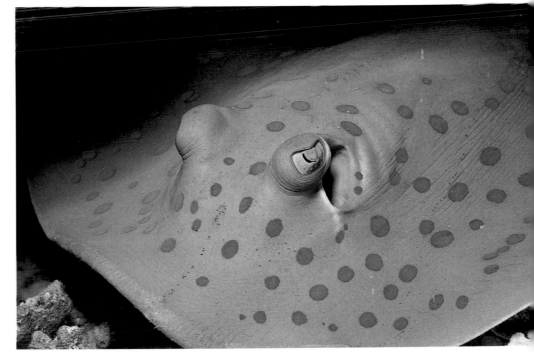

WATER BAT
As it swims, the spotted eagle ray gracefully flaps its giant fins up and down. Found in tropical seas throughout the world, the eagle ray measures up to 11 feet across, including its giant fins.

A poisonous spine near the base of the eagle ray's tail flips up to ward off enemies.

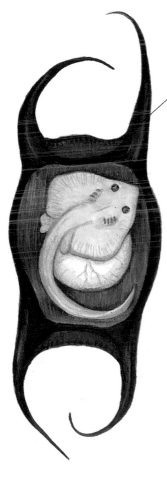

Each corner of the case has a long tendril or "horn" that helps the case attach to stones, sand, and weeds.

HEADS UP!
To take in water, rays have special openings on top of their heads. Called spiracles (SPEAR-ih-kuls), these swoosh water in, down, and out over the ray's gills. Oxygen is removed from the water as it passes over the gills.

SKATE CASE
All skates lay eggs, one to a case. The case protects the egg as the baby skate grows inside. After about a year, the young skate hatches and leaves the case.

4 Bones Are Best

Most of the world's fish are members of a large group called bony fish. They have jaws and skeletons made of bone, not cartilage. Bony fish have pairs of flexible fins, front and back, that enable them to turn and stop more easily than sharks, with their more rigid fins, can.

The fins of a coelacanth are thick and rounded like paddles.

ANCIENT RELIC
The coelacanth (SEE-luh-kanth) could win the title of the world's oldest living fish! Fossils of its ancestors date back nearly 400 million years. The coelacanth has hardly changed over time.

FISH IN THE ROUND
The roly-poly ocean sunfish can weigh as much as 1,000 pounds and reach 13 feet in length. Like most round-shaped fish, the sunfish is a poor swimmer. It spends its days lolling on its side, "sunbathing" in the open ocean.

A male black crappie uses its tail to sweep out a nest on a lake bottom where a female will lay her eggs.

NIGHT HUNTER
The black crappie comes out at night to feed on small fish or aquatic insects.

COLOR ME BLUE ▶
Bony fish include spectacular-looking coral reef dwellers, such as splashy regal tangs.

30

Long, Lean, and Lanky

If it slithers through the water like a snake, chances are it's the slippery, slinky fish known as an eel. Eels are bony fish. Unlike almost all other fish, most eels lack scales and pectoral fins. Eels come in more than 700 varieties, or species. Most live in the ocean. True to its name, the electric eel produces a shock of 600 volts, a whammy big enough to stun humans.

The garden eel secretes mucus to dig its tube-like burrow.

GARDEN GROWN
Garden eels burrow into the sandy ocean floor. Then, anchored by their tails, they rise and face into the current. They wait for tiny floating animals called zooplankton (ZOH-oh-plangk-ten) to drift by.

Their nearly transparent bodies earned elvers the name "glass eels."

HIDE AND SEEK
The brilliantly colored ribbon eel can fit its flexible, four-foot-long body into a tiny crack. During the day, the eel hides from enemies. At night, it ventures out to hunt.

WHAT'S COOKIN'?
From a rocky crevice, young fresh-water eels, or elvers, peer out at the passing scene.

MEGAMOUTH
The undulated moray eel has a mouth full of pointed teeth that help it grab octopuses and crabs. Avoid tangling with a moray. It might mistake your hand for a tasty treat.

33

Beasts With Beards

When is a fish a cat? When it's a catfish! Catfish are named for their whisker-like barbels. Most of the several thousand kinds of catfish live in fresh water. Some other kinds of fish have barbels. All live near streambeds or sea bottoms and use their barbels as feelers.

NOSE JOB
The nurse shark is one of several kinds of sharks that have barbels.

Using its pair of barbels, the nurse shark pokes around for lobsters and other shellfish.

WHICH END UP?
The upside-down catfish, found in African streams, spends much of its time upside down. From this position, the fish can easily use the barbels on its chin to sense the motion of flies on the water's surface.

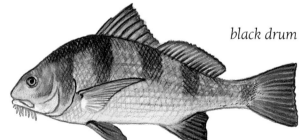

black drum

BARBED BEAUTIES
Several delicate barbels flutter from the black drum's chin. The Atlantic cod boasts a single feeler. Both fish use their barbels to explore the ocean bottom for food.

Atlantic cod

SPINES AND STRIPES ▶
Young striped eel catfish gather around coral reefs in warm oceans. Their stripes warn enemies of danger. If a predator comes too close, this catfish often zaps it with poisonous spines located near its fins.

34

5 Watery Worlds

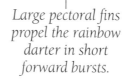

Fish have shown an awesome ability to fit in, or adapt, to a variety of watery homes or habitats. A freshwater fish may have large fins to help it snag a meal in fast-moving streams. An ocean dweller that lives in a coral reef may have colors that blend with the reef, hiding it from enemies; creatures of the dark ocean depths may have built-in lights.

Large pectoral fins propel the rainbow darter in short forward bursts.

FAST MOVERS
You'd have a tough time if you went looking for the rainbow darter. Only three inches long—and shy—it hides on the bottom of fast-flowing creeks and rivers.

IT'S A GEM
The African jewelfish, a type of fish called a cichlid (SIK-lid), dwells in fresh water. Several hundred different kinds of cichlids may live in a single African lake.

LAKE LIFE ▶
Clear, deep lakes provide a variety of habitats for fish. Generally, particular fish favor one or two habitats. Some go back and forth between deep water and shallow, resting in one spot and feeding in another. Big fish often eat smaller ones, while little fish feed on insects or microscopic animals.

IN THE NOSE
There are only two kinds of freshwater paddlefish. One swims in rivers in the central United States, the other in the Yangtze River of China.

The oar-like snout of the paddlefish grows to a third of the fish's three-to-seven-foot length.

black crappie

golden shiners

bluegill

muskellunge

largemouth bass

emerald shiners

yellow perch

walleye

lake trout

burbot

37

Underwater Apartment

In warm and shallow oceans, fish in dazzling colors dart in and out of coral reefs. Reefs form over hundreds of years as skeletons of millions of tiny animals called coral polyps (POL-EHPS) build underwater ridges. A reef is like a sunken apartment building, providing food and shelter for as many as 400 kinds of fish, as well as other animals and plants. Each species makes the most of its habitat—feeding, resting, reproducing, and hiding in and around the reef.

The harlequin tuskfish crunches shellfish with its sharp, tusk-like teeth.

TELLTALE TEETH
The lower incisors of the harlequin tuskfish stick out so much that this fish has an underbite! Spotting shellfish hidden in a crevice, the tuskfish uses its strong jaws and teeth to haul out prey and devour it.

SPOTS 'N SQUARES
On a bright coral reef, a longnose hawkfish boasts the same orange-and-red colors as its surroundings. Nearly invisible, the hawkfish lies in wait to strike at passing prey.

SKINNY MINNIE
The pencil-shaped trumpetfish hangs head down. It looks like a piece of coral on the reef.

SNOOZE ON!

Ready for a rest, a redband parrotfish settles near the reef floor. Here, it is hard to spot behind an orange sponge and blue-gray coral.

The thin, plate-shaped body of the black velvet angelfish helps it turn on a dime in tight spots.

MADE TO MOVE

The flat, flexible bodies of angelfish allow them to slip between plant stems and coral formations.

Creeps of the Deep

Several miles below the surface, the ocean is pitch black and freezing cold. Food is scarce. Only a little light filters down from above. Still, more than 2,000 kinds of fish dwell in this unfriendly habitat. Some have special light organs or body parts that help them survive in this world. Many look like monsters, but most are small, rarely reaching a foot in length.

The silver scales of a deep-sea hatchetfish dazzle enemies.

HATCHET MAN

Only three inches long, a hatchetfish sends a quick flash from its light organ that blinds an enemy and gives the hatchetfish a chance to dash to safety.

WATER DRAGON

Bright lights line the body of a dragonfish. Mimicking faint rays of sunlight, the fish's lights may confuse enemies below.

A dragonfish wiggles its lighted barbel to attract prey.

DEEP INTO LIFE

The built-in lights of many deep-sea creatures occur as a result of chemical reactions in the cells inside the fish. These cells are either part of the fish or belong to organisms called bacteria (back-TIER-ee-ah). Certain types of bacteria live and make light inside the fish. The lights may confuse enemies or attract prey. Some lights may help male and female fish of the same kind find each other.

deep-sea gulper eel

40

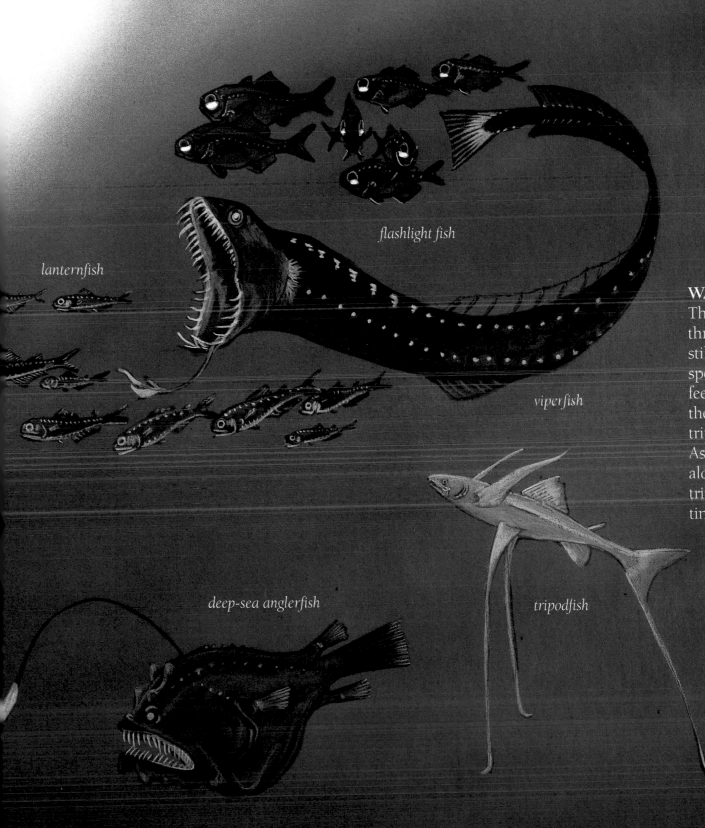

flashlight fish

lanternfish

viperfish

WALKING TALL
The tripodfish uses its
three long fins like
stilts. The fins have
special sensory, or
feeling, organs on
them that help the
tripodfish find supper.
As it drags its fins
along the bottom, a
tripodfish can feel the
tiniest bit of food.

deep-sea anglerfish

tripodfish

41

6 Working Together

Some fish live in close harmony with another kind of animal. Often, the choice of partner seems odd. What fish would want to be pals with a stinging sea anemone? Strange as they may seem, the pairings usually help both partners. This type of relationship, which benefits both animals, is called mutualism (MYOO-chew-eh-LIZ-em).

The tiny cleaner wrasse serves as a toothbrush for a grouper.

GOOD GUY, BAD GUY

The cleaner wrasse performs a valuable service for many larger fish. It moves over them, eating diseased tissue, itchy bacteria, or parasites. To advertise its services, the cleaner wrasse wriggles invitingly. The mimic blenny looks and acts like the cleaner wrasse, but when a large fish approaches, the blenny takes a bite.

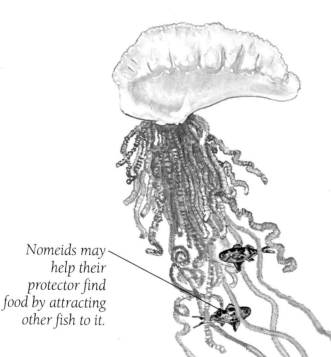

Nomeids may help their protector find food by attracting other fish to it.

The small mimi[c] blenny attacks [a] parrotfish.

TUCKED AMONG TENTACLES

The man-of-war fish, or nomeid (no-MEE-id), is immune to the poisonous tentacles of the jellyfish-like Portuguese man-of-war. Nomeid young seek protection from attackers among the man-of-war's tentacles.

PLAYING PEEKABOO ▶

A clownfish, or anemonefish (eh-NEM-eh-nee-fish), wears a coat of mucus that lets it live unharmed within the stinging tentacles of the sea anemone, a relative of the jellyfish. The clownfish hides from enemies and chases away fish that might nibble the anemone's tentacles.

7 Don't Mess With Me!

Fish defend themselves in a wide variety of ways. To escape attack, some find safety in numbers, swimming in schools. Others hide by blending with their environment. Some fish zap an enemy or other fish with powerful electrical charges, and some have poisonous spines or other projections that repel predators.

Poison in the spiny rays of a lionfish's fins can cripple an attacker.

SERIOUS STRIPES
To warn away enemies, the reef-dwelling lionfish flutters its poisonous fins as it swims.

LIKE A ROCK
Resting on the bottom of a warm sea, a stonefish is nearly invisible. Buried spines in its back inject poison into anything that touches it.

44

BORN TO BE BAD

Armed with a mouthful of razor-sharp teeth, the barracuda is a fearsome predator of tropical seas. It attacks small fish and has come after people, too.

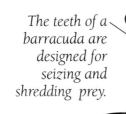

The teeth of a barracuda are designed for seizing and shredding prey.

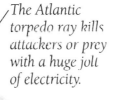

The Atlantic torpedo ray kills attackers or prey with a huge jolt of electricity.

EATING MACHINES

Sharp teeth and strong jaws enable redbellied piranhas, found in South America's fresh waters, to strip their prey of flesh in just minutes.

8 Funny Forms

Most fish have a familiar "fishy" shape. You'd know them as fish anywhere. Others have weird shapes. They look like floating plates, swimming porcupines, or tiny horse-headed aliens, yet these strangely shaped creatures are fish. Over time fish have developed particular forms to help them survive. A fish's shape helps it find food and escape attack.

A long, curving snout helps the elephantfish poke the mud in African lakes and rivers looking for foo[d]

HORSE OF ANOTHER COLOR

A seahorse can change color to match its surroundings, and its strange shape helps the seahorse blend in with seaweed or coral. The seahorse anchors itself with its tail and waits to suck in tiny animals that swim by.

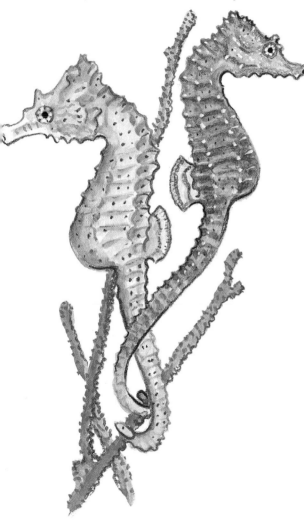

A boxfish's spots warn enemies not to mess with it. The fish secretes a deadly mucus.

FISH-IN-A-BOX

Flat, bony plates give the Hawaiian boxfish a rectangular shape that inspired its name. The plates protect this slow-moving ocean fish.

A SPEEDING BULLET

Fastest fish in the sea, the sailfish is shaped like a torpedo for speed. Sailfish have been clocked going nearly 70 miles an hour. In the open sea, speed is essential for catching prey.

PRICKLY CHARACTER

When threatened, a porcupinefish gulps in air or water. Its body balloons, raising prickly spines that repel would-be attackers. What animal would want to dine on a pincushion?

47

Quick-change Artists

Some fish pull off an amazing feat. They begin life in one form, then change into another. Halibut, sole, and the 500 kinds of fish known as flatfish all change shape. At birth, a flatfish has a familiar fishy shape. Soon its body starts to flatten out, and one eye moves across the top of its head to the other side. Once flattened, these fish settle onto the ocean floor and lie in wait to ambush passing prey.

CAMOUFLAGE COLORS
Like most flounders, the summer flounder changes skin pattern and color to hide amid its surroundings. This species of flounder got its name because it is common in the coastal waters of the Atlantic Ocean during the summer.

FLOUNDERING AROUND
When feeding, or when it is disturbed, the winter flounder rises from the seafloor and swims off. The fish was named because it is found along much of the Atlantic coast during the winter.

This winter flounder's eyes are on its right side. Those of a summer flounder are on the left.

"PANCAKE" MAKING

It takes about five weeks for a baby flounder to complete its transformation. The flounder's left eye moves across its head. Its jaw and skull change, too, so that the right side of its head becomes the top. When fully flattened, the flounder nestles down to a life on the ocean floor.

What Fish?

Life in the sea is dangerous. Fish prey on each other. Birds—from gulls to eagles—and mammals, such as bears and seals, eat fish. A fish's color or pattern can help it hide from such enemies. Fish mix and match colors in various ways. Some disguise themselves another way. They are colorless, which makes them nearly invisible to predators and can also help them catch prey.

HIDDEN TREASURE
The blue-green hues and pencil shape of a pipefish help it hide while resting upright among sea grasses.

The fan-shaped dorsal fins of a twinspot goby have black spots that look like the eyes of a crab.

SEE ME?
Wavy white lines on a filefish imitate its surroundings so well that it can hide from danger in the delicate arms of a feather star, a cousin of the sea urchin.

LEAF ME ALONE ▶
Drifting down a stream, the Amazon leaf fish could fool almost any predator or prey. Its markings, including a stem-like barbel on its chin, help it look like a leaf.

50

Now You See It, Now You Don't

Color helps fish of the same species recognize each other. Males, which are often brighter than females, use color to attract mates. Fish also use color to defend themselves. Some fish have spots like eyes on their tails or fins. A predator can confuse these false eyes for the fish's real ones and attack the fakes, giving its prey time to dart away.

ALL CLEAR
The body of the glass catfish helps i
defend itself. The body is
transparent, making the fish almost
invisible to predators.

The young of many angelfish, such as the emperor, are colored differently than the adults. Circles and lines on a young emperor angelfish may make it hard to spot.

THE ANGLE ON ANGELFISH
Each kind of angelfish sports its own combination of patterned patches, dots, and bars, probably so that it can recognize its own kind.

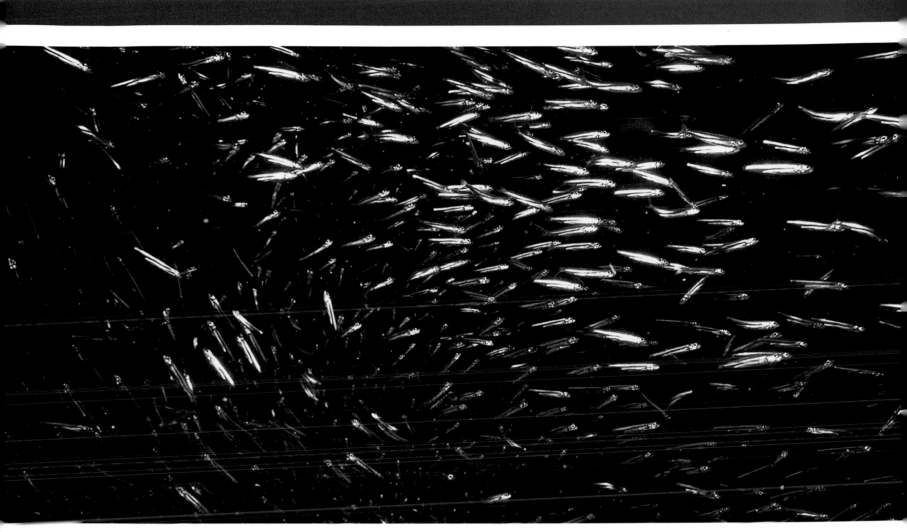

FISH SCHOOL
In the open ocean, a huge school of anchovies swims near the surface. From below, where predators lurk, the silvery sides of the anchovies sparkle like rays of light. A would-be attacker might mistake the fish for flashes of sunlight.

Its coloring helps the shield darter hide in the gravel of streambeds.

MALL BUT SWIFT
Only three inches ong, the shield darter wells on the bottoms f fast-moving creeks nd rivers.

9 Fishy Fish

You probably think of most fish as streamlined swimmers that live in water, but that's not always the case. Some fish are lumpy and warty and can even "walk" on their fins. Others can live out of the water for long periods. Several kinds of fish appear to "fly." One type climbs around on mudflats. Clearly, fish have many hidden talents!

FISH OUT OF WATER
When the ponds they live in disappear in the African dry season, lungfish crawl out of the water and build mud burrows where they hibernate for several months. Lungfish have lungs as well as gills, so they can live in or out of water.

A SKIP OR A JUMP?
Low tide in Southeast Asia's mangrove swamps finds a mudskipper hopping across the ground on its strong fins. The mudskipper gulps in a lot of water to keep its gills moist before it makes a leap onto land.

With fins like legs, the frogfish can "walk" on the seafloor. Frogfish live in tropical seas.

54

The pectoral fins of a flying fish resemble wings.

IT'S A BIRD…

The flying fish doesn't actually fly. It beats its tail back and forth to build up speed, then leaps out of the water, fans out its pectoral fins, and glides through the air.

MAJOR UGLY? NOT!

Large body flaps and warts, plus the ability to change color, help a frogfish blend with its surroundings.

Did You Know...

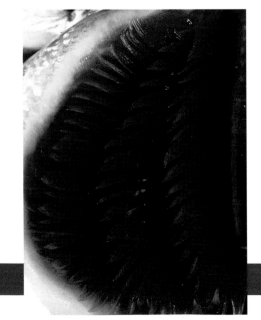

1 **THAT** there are about 40 different kinds of blind and colorless fish? Like this cavefish, they are adapted to dark places. In a totally black environment, these fish don't need to see. Instead of eyes, they have sensing organs that help them feel when a predator or prey is near.

2 **THAT** the male sockeye salmon changes its looks? Just before breeding, his greenish-blue coloring turns a brilliant red, and his head becomes a deep green. His back becomes humped, and his upper jaw hooks over his lower one. These changes let a female know the male sockeye is ready to mate.

3 **THAT** fish gills, like this one from a salmon, are red because of all the blood in them? A fish's blood takes in, or absorbs, oxygen from the water and carries it throughout the fish's body.

4 **THAT** the parrotfish has teeth that look like a beak? Those beaky teeth inspired the name "parrotfish." Found only on tropical reefs, parrotfish use their teeth to scrape corals for food. Divers can hear the crunching a group of feeding parrotfish makes long before they see the animals.

5 **THAT** several kinds of rays have poisonous spines near the base of their tails? When attacked, the ray raises its tail and pushes up a spine. The resulting wound, though painful, is rarely fatal to large animals. Some sharks have been found swimming around with broken ray spines in their mouths and stomachs.

6 **THAT** male seahorses have babies? A female seahorse lays as many as 200 eggs in a pouch on the stomach of the male. At birthing time, the male seahorse coils his tail around a weed and jerks back and forth until the tiny fish pop out of his pouch.

Glossary

ADAPT To change over the ages in response to a certain environment or set of conditions.

BACTERIA Tiny, one-celled organisms found in the bodies of fish, as well as in other animals, organic matter, plants, soil, and air.

BARBEL A slender feeler on or near the mouths of some kinds of fish.

CARTILAGE Strong, flexible material that makes up the skeletons of some fish, such as jawless fish, skates, and rays.

CICHLID Any of a family of tropical freshwater fish that are often brightly colored.

COELACANTH Any of several large fish, once thought to be extinct, whose ancestors lived nearly 400 million years ago.

COLD-BLOODED Having a body temperature that varies with the temperature of the surroundings.

CRUSTACEAN An animal with a hard shell and a jointed body and legs that lives mostly in the water, such as a crab, a lobster, and a shrimp.

DENTICLES Tooth-like projections covering a shark's skin.

GILLS The organs of fish and other creatures that take in oxygen from the water.

MOLLUSK A soft-bodied animal that lacks a backbone and is not divided into segments. A mollusk is sometimes covered with a hard shell, such as a clam.

MUTUALISM A relationship between two living things from which each benefits.

OPERCULUM The covering of a fish's gills.

PARASITE An organism that lives on or in another life form; a parasite gets its food from its host and often harms it.

PREDATOR An animal that hunts and kills other animals for food.

PREY An animal that is hunted by other animals for food.

PROTEIN The main chemical material found in all living cells that contains carbon, hydrogen, nitrogen, and oxygen.

SCALE One of the small, flattened, hard plates that make up the outer skin of fish, reptiles, and the legs of birds.

SCHOOL A large number of the same kind of fish or other aquatic animals swimming together.

SHELLFISH A shelled aquatic animal, such as an oyster, clam, crab, or lobster, that is eaten by people.

SPECIES A group of animals of the same kind that can produce young like themselves.

SPAWNING The act of reproducing young fish, generally in large numbers.

VERTEBRATE An animal—fish, amphibian, reptile, bird, or mammal—with a backbone.

ZOOPLANKTON Tiny animals that drift in water.

Credits

copperband butterfly fish

Published by
The National Geographic Society
Reg Murphy, *President*
 and Chief Executive Officer
Gilbert M. Grosvenor,
 Chairman of the Board
Nina D. Hoffman,
 Senior Vice President
William R. Gray, *Vice President and Director, Book Division*

Staff for this Book
Barbara Lalicki, *Director of Children's Publishing*
Barbara Brownell, *Senior Editor and Project Manager*
Marianne R. Koszorus, *Senior Art Director and Project Manager*
Toni Eugene, *Editor*
Alexandra Littlehales, *Art Director*
Sally Collins, *Illustrations Editor*
Elizabeth Schleichert, *Researcher*
Meredith Wilcox, *Illustrations Assistant*
Dale-Marie Herring, *Administrative Assistant*
Elisabeth MacRae-Bobynskyj, *Indexer*
Mark A. Caraluzzi, *Marketing Manager*
Vincent P. Ryan, *Manufacturing Manager*

Acknowledgments

We are grateful for the assistance of Valerie Chase, Ph.D., Staff
Biologist, National Aquarium in Baltimore, *Scientific Consultant.*
We also thank John Agnone and Rebecca Lescaze, National
Geographic Book Division, for their guidance and suggestions.

Illustrations Credits

Cover: David Doubilet.
Interior photos from Animals Animals/Earth Scenes:
Front Matter: 1 Zig Leszczynski. 2-3 W. Gregory Brown. 4 (top to bottom), Carl Roessler; Keith Ringland/OSF; Zig Leszczynski; Max Gibbs/OSF. 5 (top to bottom), Steven David Miller; W. Gregory Brown; James D. Watt; Zig Leszczynski; Max Gibbs/OSF. 6-7 (art), Warren Cutler. 8-9 E.R. Degginger. 10 (art), Robert Cremins; 10 James D. Watt. 11 (art), Robert Cremins. 11 Gérard Lacz. 12 (art), Robert Cremins. 12 (upper), Gérard Lacz; (lower), Zig Leszczynski. 13 Gérard Lacz. 14 (art), Warren Cutler. 14-15 Ashod Francis. 15 (art), Robert Cremins. 15 (upper), Carl Roessler; (lower), Waina Cheng/OSF. 16 (art), Robert Cremins. 16 (left), Breck P. Kent; (right) Zig Leszczynski. 17 (both), Gérard Lacz.
Life Cycle: 18-19 (all), Mark Stouffer. 20 Keith Ringland/OSF. 21 (art), Warren Cutler.
Jawless Fish: 22 (art, both), Robert Cremins. 22 Zig Leszczynski. 23 John Paling/OSF.
Sharks, Rays, and Skates: 24 (art), Robert Cremins. 24 (upper), G.I. Bernard; (lower), R. Ingo Riepl. 25 Carl Roessler. 26-27 (art), Warren Cutler. 27 (center), James D. Watt. 27 (lower), Carl Roessler. 28 (art), Robert Cremins. 28 Doug Wechsler. 29 (art), Warren Cutler. 29 (upper), Zig Leszczynski; (lower), W. Gregory Brown.
Bony Fish: 30 (art, left), Warren Cutler; (art, right), Robert Cremins. 30 L.L.T. Rhodes. 30-31 Max Gibbs/OSF. 32 (art), Robert Cremins. 32 (left), Zig Leszczynski; (right), Rodger Jackman/OSF. 33 Fritz Prenzel. 34 (art), Warren Cutler. 34 (left), L.L.T. Rhodes; (right), Miriam Austerman. 35 Ashod Francis.
Habitats: 36 (upper), Raymond A. Mendez; (center), Mella Panzella; (lower), Doug Wechsler. 37 (art), Warren Cutler. 38 (art), Robert Cremins. 38 (upper), Steven David Miller; (lower), James D. Watt 39 (upper), W. Gregory Brown; (lower), Zig Leszczynski. 40 (both), OSF. 40-41 (art), Warren Cutler.
Mutualism: 42 (art, left), Warren Cutler; (art, right), Robert Cremins. 42 W. Gregory Brown 43 Bruce Watkins.
Defense Mechanisms: 44 (upper), Zig Leszczynski; (lower), Carl Roessler. 45 (art), Robert Cremins. 45 (upper), James D. Watt; (lower), Mella Panzella.
Forms of Fish: 46 (art), Robert Cremins. 46 Howard Hall/OSF. 47 (art), Warren Cutler. 47 (upper), Zig Leszczynski; (lower), Bruce Watkins. 48 (upper), Herb Segars; (lower), Ted Levin. 49 (art), Warren Cutler. 50 (art), Robert Cremins. 50 (left), W. Gregory Brown; (right), Zig Leszczynski. 51-52 (all), Zig Leszczynski. 53 (art), Robert Cremins. 53 C.C. Lockwood.
Fishy Fish: 54 (art), Robert Cremins. 54, Zig Leszczynski. 54-55 Max Gibbs/OSF. 55 Peter Parks/OSF.
Back Matter: 56 (art), Robert Cremins. 56 (upper), Breck P. Kent; (lower), G.I. Bernard. 57 (art), Warren Cutler. 57 (both), Zig Leszczynski. 60 Zig Leszczynski.

COVER: A reef-dwelling clownfish, immune to the stings of a sea anemone, finds safety from predators among its waving tentacles.

Composition for this book by the National Geographic Society Book Division. Printed and bound by R.R. Donnelley & Sons Company, Willard, Ohio. Color separations by NEC, Nashville, Tennessee. Case cover printed by Inland Press, Menomonee Falls, Wisconsin.

Library of Congress CIP Data
Schleichert, Elizabeth
     Fish / by Elizabeth Schleichert.
          p.   cm — (National Geographic nature library)
     Includes index.
     Summary: Discusses the physical differences of fish and
examines different kinds, including sharks, eels, and catfish.
     ISBN 0-7922-7043-6
     1.Fishes—Juvenile literature.   [1.Fishes.]   I. Title.
II. Series.
     QL617.2S34   1997
     597—dc21
                                                                      97-14563
                                                                        CIP
                                                                        AC